Science Close-Up®

FOSSILS

Written by Robert A. Bell
Illustrated by James Spence

A GOLDEN BOOK • NEW YORK
Western Publishing Company, Inc., Racine, Wisconsin 53404

© 1992 Western Publishing Company, Inc. Illustrations © 1992 James Spence. All rights reserved.
Printed in the U.S.A. No part of this book may be reproduced or copied in any form without
written permission from the publisher. All trademarks are the property of Western Publishing
Company, Inc. Library of Congress Catalog Card Number: 92-70368   ISBN: 0-307-12855-5
A   MCMXCII

The Terrible Lizard

More than 150 years ago, English workmen were digging rocks out of the ground to use as building material. Instead, they found the strangest objects they had ever seen buried in the earth.

What they uncovered were **fossil** bones, or bones that had turned to stone. They were the bones of an animal— the biggest animal anybody had ever seen.

The workers carefully cut the fossils from the rock. Scientists later pieced the bones together into an animal fifteen feet high with giant teeth and long, sharp claws. It was like nothing else on earth.

One scientist, Richard Owen, made up a name for this monster, using Latin words that meant "terrible lizard." Owen's name for the animal was *dinosaur*.

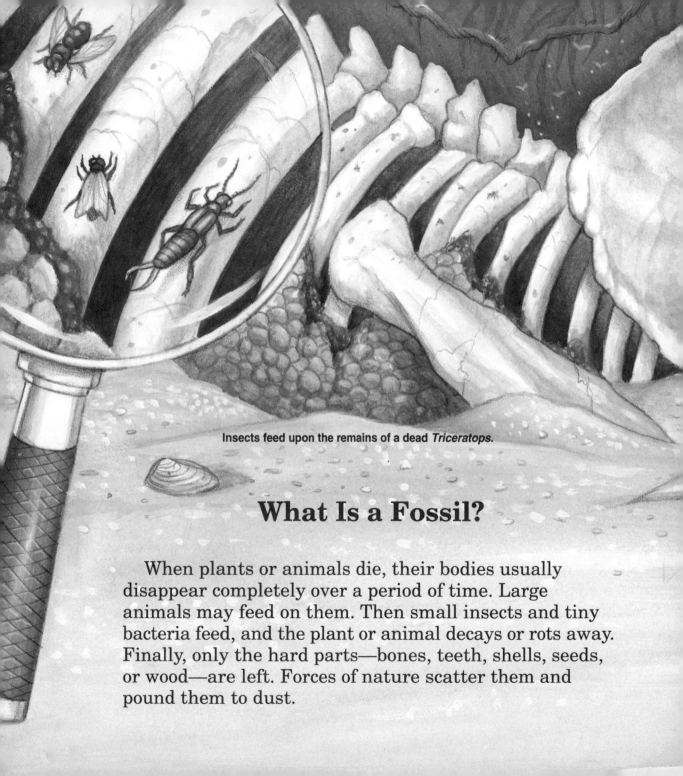

Insects feed upon the remains of a dead *Triceratops*.

What Is a Fossil?

When plants or animals die, their bodies usually disappear completely over a period of time. Large animals may feed on them. Then small insects and tiny bacteria feed, and the plant or animal decays or rots away. Finally, only the hard parts—bones, teeth, shells, seeds, or wood—are left. Forces of nature scatter them and pound them to dust.

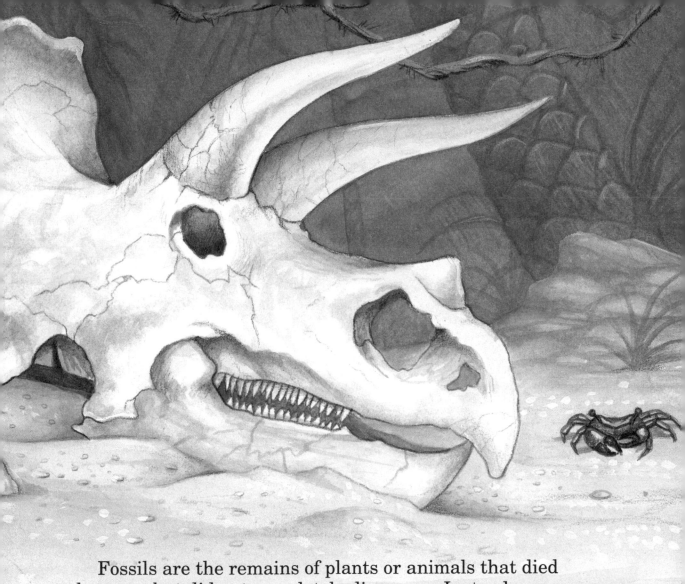

Fossils are the remains of plants or animals that died long ago but did not completely disappear. Instead, some of their remains were saved from decay and slowly turned to stone—all by accidents of nature.

These accidents are lucky for us. Fossils are like magic windows that allow us to look far back in time. They have amazing stories to tell about life in the distant past.

body of dinosaur being covered by sand

Megalosaurus

The Making of a Fossil

The fifteen-foot monster that Richard Owen named *dinosaur* died millions of years ago. We don't know why it died. Maybe it was sickness or old age. Maybe another dinosaur killed it for food. One thing we do know is that it was covered by sand and mud soon after it died.

Beneath the sand, bacteria and other tiny creatures fed on the dinosaur. Soon only the bones were left. Covered as they were, the bones stayed in one place. Wind and weather could not scatter them and pound them to dust.

Year after year, rains came and washed more mud and sand over the bones. The earth piled higher and higher. Over time, deep in the earth, an amazing thing began to happen.

bones beneath the earth

Turning Bone into Stone

Very slowly the dinosaur bones began to change. *Molecules* from the minerals in the sand and mud began to enter the bones. (Molecules are groups of *atoms*. Atoms are the tiny pieces from which everything in the world is made.) One by one, these mineral molecules took the place of the molecules of bone. One molecule at a time, the bones turned into minerals—into stone.

It took many thousands of years, but the pieces of stone that remained were the exact shape and size of the dinosaur's bones.

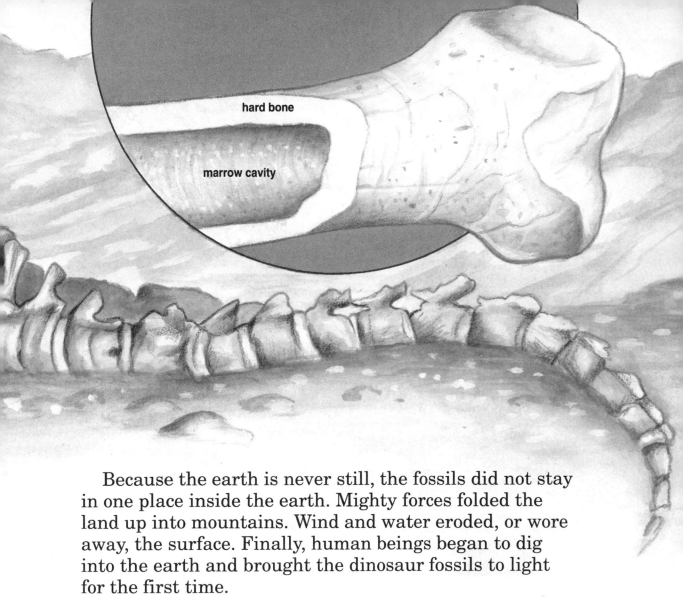

Because the earth is never still, the fossils did not stay in one place inside the earth. Mighty forces folded the land up into mountains. Wind and water eroded, or wore away, the surface. Finally, human beings began to dig into the earth and brought the dinosaur fossils to light for the first time.

The fossil bones of dinosaurs are just one of thousands of different kinds of fossils that you can see today. When examining a specimen of dinosaur bone, look for small circles. These show where the *marrow* structure in the bone was. (Marrow is the soft center part of bones.)

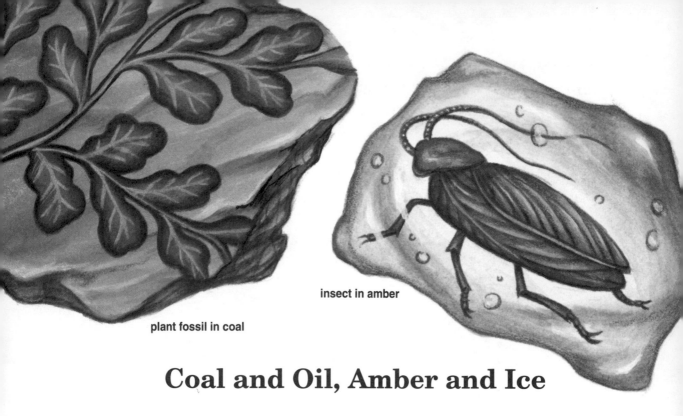

insect in amber

plant fossil in coal

Coal and Oil, Amber and Ice

Most of the fossils that have been found are either bones or some hard part of boneless animals or plants. But another kind of fossil is one that shows the *impression,* or shape, of a living thing. Many footprints of ancient animals or people have become fossilized. Also, the leaves and stems of ancient plants and the bodies of small animals have left impressions in mud, which then turned to solid rock.

Oil and coal, which are called *fossil fuels,* are formed from animals and plants that died long ago. Deep underground, heat and pressure have changed the remains into fuel that we use to heat our homes and run our cars every day.

Sometimes lucky accidents of nature have saved whole plants or animals from the distant past without changing them at all. Amber is a clear, yellowish stone. The stones began as balls of sticky tree sap in which insects sometimes became trapped. Pieces of amber have been found with perfect prehistoric insect bodies inside.

In some cases, animals in early times fell into pits full of black sticky tar, and were preserved in it. And in Siberia, *woolly mammoths*—a kind of ancient, hairy elephant—have been found completely frozen in ice!

woolly mammoth frozen in ice

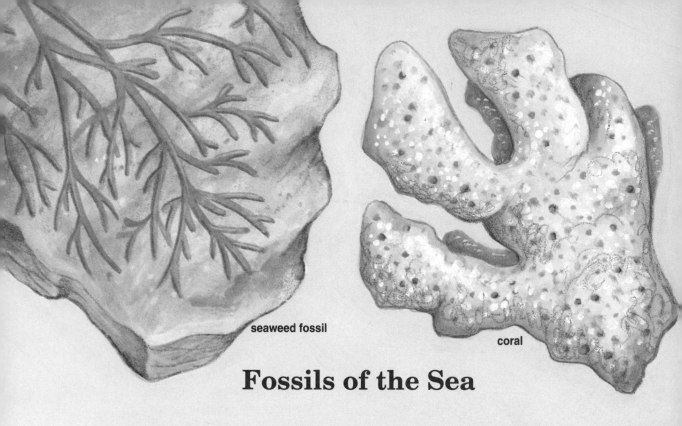

seaweed fossil

coral

Fossils of the Sea

Life first appeared in the ocean. And living things have made the ocean their home for hundreds of millions of years.

The sea is full of plants called **algae**. Some algae are too small to see, while others are much larger. You probably know the large ones as seaweed. Fossil impressions of algae show that they are among the oldest of all plants.

The world's warm seas are also filled with **coral** reefs. Coral is a tiny, very simple animal. The reefs are made up of their hard outer shells—millions of shells at a time. Coral has also been on earth for a long time. Fossil coral over 400 million years old has been found.

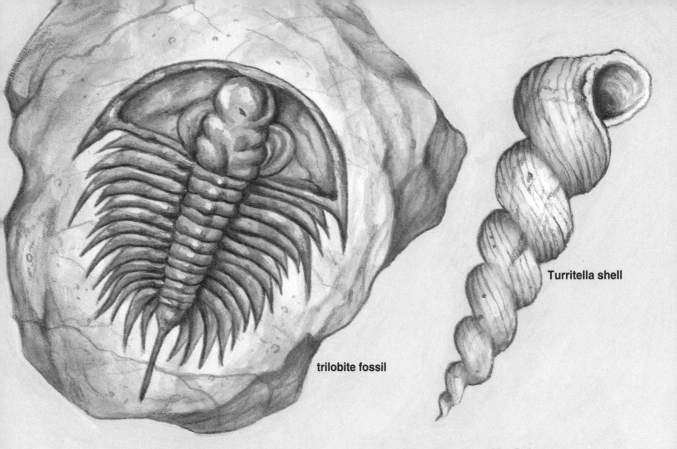

trilobite fossil

Turritella shell

Algae and coral live in the seas today. But **trilobites** —once-abundant creatures that crawled on the sea bottom like lobsters and crabs—are now found *only* as fossils. Appearing about 550 million years ago, trilobites became extinct, or died out, about 200 million years ago. Today, only their relatives—lobsters, crabs, and many insects—remain.

Many other extinct sea creatures—including **Turritellas,** which were snaillike bottom dwellers—are also found as fossils. In a specimen of Turritella, look for winding patterns, which are the preserved parts of the animal's shell.

Fossils of the Air

About 270 million years ago, a gigantic insect flew through the deep, silent forests. It looked like today's dragonfly—but seven times bigger! *Meganeura* had a wingspread of more than two feet. The delicate wings left impressions in stone when *Meganeura* became a fossil.

Meganeura

Archaeopteryx

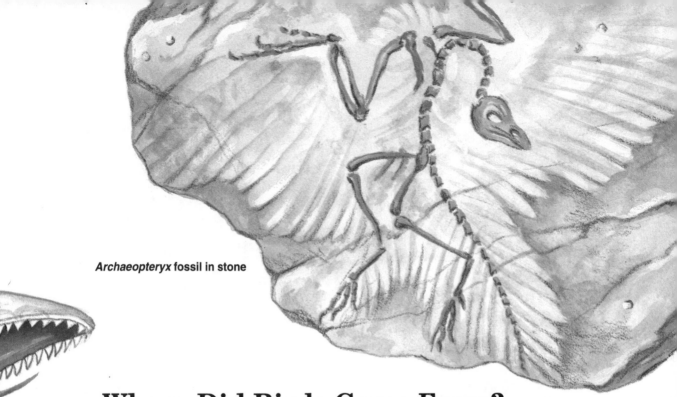

Archaeopteryx fossil in stone

Where Did Birds Come From?

For many years, scientists wondered where birds came from. They knew that birds must have evolved—changed slowly over time—from an earlier creature. But which one? And when? No one knew until 1877, when the fossil skeleton of *Archaeopteryx* was found.

Archaeopteryx was a strange creature. Like a bird, it had wings and a beak. The impression of feathers shows clearly in the fossils we have. But it had teeth, and its skeleton was clearly related to that of a dinosaur and the reptile group to which dinosaurs belong.

Archaeopteryx became the world's most famous fossil. It proved that birds evolved from reptiles between 70 and 100 million years ago.

tree fern

giant club moss

Fossils of the Land

About 300 million years ago, North America was covered with thick forests full of trees and ferns, bushes and moss. By studying fossil impressions, we have learned that many of them were like plants today. But there were also plants that have since become extinct, like the **giant club moss** and the **tree fern**.

Unlike many soft plants, trees are hard enough to become fossils. We call fossil trees **petrified wood**. If you look closely at petrified wood, you can see the long wood fibers etched in the stone. It is rougher than the smooth surface of bone.

cross section of petrified wood

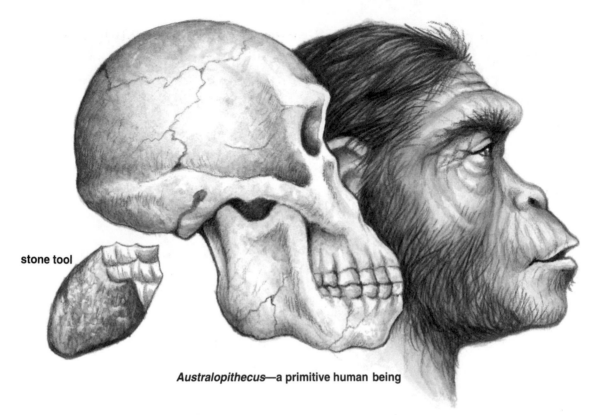

stone tool

Australopithecus—a primitive human being

What Do Fossils Tell Us?

Fossils let us know about some of the most important things that happened in the past. Fossil bones of human beings, as well as the remains of artifacts and tools, have survived to tell us the story of our earliest beginnings.

It is only because of the fossils we have found that we know dinosaurs were the biggest creatures on earth for nearly 130 million years. Until the workmen in England discovered the first giant fossil bones, we didn't even know dinosaurs had ever existed.

Fossils also show us how living things change. Because of fossils, we know that one kind of plant or animal slowly gives rise to another. *Archaeopteryx* developed from reptiles and, in turn, evolved into true birds. An animal named *Eohippus* that lived 60 million years ago was the ancestor of today's horse. The woolly mammoths that first walked the earth 7 million years ago are gone, and today's elephants have taken their place.

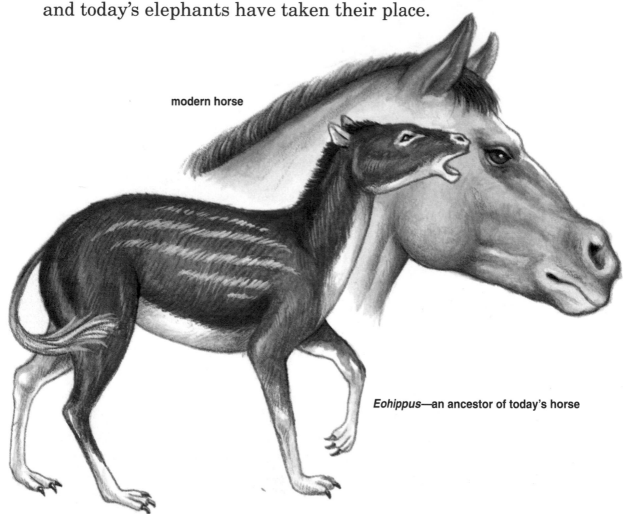

modern horse

Eohippus—an ancestor of today's horse

a desert in the American Southwest
once covered by an ocean

Fossil Maps

Fossils also tell us what different areas of the earth were like long ago.

In certain places, North America has huge amounts of underground coal. We know that coal forms in warm climates. Because of the coal deposits, we know that most of North America was hot and humid about 250 million years ago.

In places where algae and coral fossils are found, we can be certain that the land was covered by a warm sea millions of years ago. The great desert of the American West is full of the fossils of sea creatures. Because of these fossils, we can be sure that 150 million years ago Colorado, Utah, New Mexico, and Arizona were covered by an ocean. Scientists have named this ancient ocean the Sundance Sea.

marine animals in the Sundance Sea

Triceratops

Cretaceous Period
135–65 million years ago

Apatosaurus

Jurassic Period
180–135 million years ago

Sphenophyllum plant

Plateosaurus

Triassic Period
225–180 million years ago

Fossil Clocks

Fossils also tell us *when* things happened long ago. The rocks where fossils are found are like a layer cake. Many different layers are piled on top of each other. Each layer shows where sand, dirt, and mud piled up and then were squeezed into stone by the weight of the layers above them. The upper layers of rock are younger, and the lower ones are older.

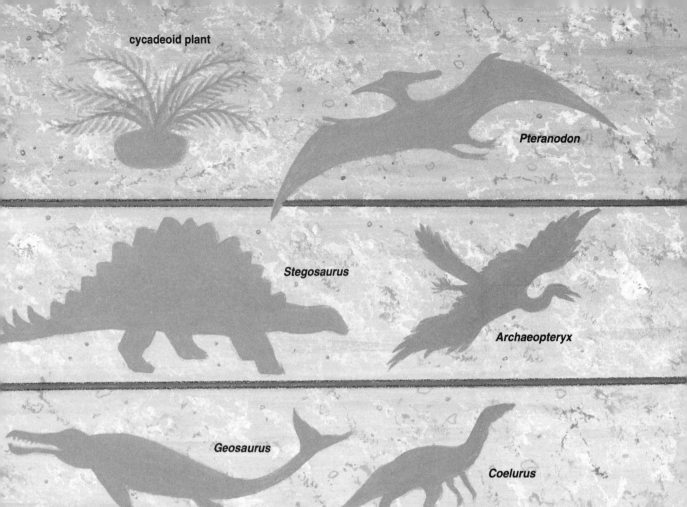

cycadeoid plant

Pteranodon

Stegosaurus

Archaeopteryx

Geosaurus

Coelurus

By careful study, scientists can usually tell when each rock layer was formed. When a fossil is found in one particular layer of rock, we have a fairly good idea how old it is. Even more important, we can tell in what order the living things of the past evolved. We are certain that life began in the sea. And we know that animals with four legs first crawled onto land about 400 million years ago.

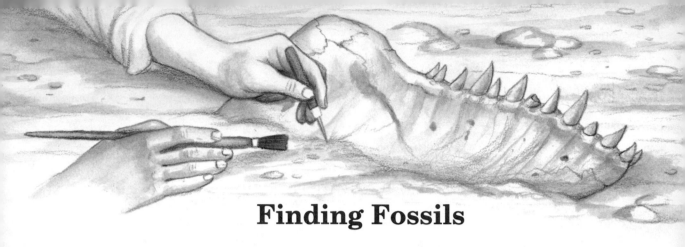

Finding Fossils

Wind and weather slowly erode rock, wearing it away. As rocks erode, fossils are uncovered. Because of this, scientists hunt for fossils wherever bare rock is found: in desert canyons, along riverbanks, and in mines and quarries.

Small fossils are sometimes found in rocks that are lying loose on the ground. Large ones must be carefully cut from the rock where they are embedded. Scientists who work too fast risk cutting the fossil itself!

Once it is dug up, a newly discovered fossil goes to a laboratory for more precise cutting and cleaning. Finally, the fossil may end up in a museum collection. A natural history museum near you may have a fossil collection. Or you can visit one of the museums listed below.

California
San Diego: San Diego Natural History Museum

Colorado
Denver: Denver Museum of Natural History

Connecticut
New Haven: Peabody Museum, Yale University

Illinois
Chicago: Field Museum of Natural History

New York
New York City: American Museum of Natural History

Washington, D.C.
Smithsonian Institution